AF228484

DODGE CHARGER

Elsie Olson

Big Buddy Books

An Imprint of Abdo Publishing
abdobooks.com

abdobooks.com

Published by Abdo Publishing, a division of ABDO, PO Box 398166, Minneapolis, Minnesota 55439. Copyright © 2021 by Abdo Consulting Group, Inc. International copyrights reserved in all countries. No part of this book may be reproduced in any form without written permission from the publisher. Big Buddy Books™ is a trademark and logo of Abdo Publishing.

Printed in the United States of America, North Mankato, Minnesota
082020
012021

Design: Christa Schneider, Mighty Media, Inc.
Production: Mighty Media, Inc.
Editor: Megan Borgert-Spaniol

Cover Photograph: Stephen Smith/AP Images

Interior Photographs: AlfvanBeem/Wikimedia Commons, p. 28 (1968); Angela2109/
    Wikimedia Commons, p. 29 (1982); FCA US LLC/Flickr, pp. 26, 27; Greg Gjerdingen/
    Wikimedia Commons, pp. 16, 17; John Lloyd/Flickr, pp. 12, 13; Library of Congress, p. 9;
    Shutterstock Images, pp. 4, 5, 7, 14, 15, 19, 20, 21, 24, 25, 28, 29; Sicnag/Wikimedia
    Commons, pp. 11, 22, 23

Design Elements: Shutterstock Images

Library of Congress Control Number: 2020931627

Publisher's Cataloging-in-Publication Data
Names: Olson, Elsie, author.
Title: Dodge Charger / by Elsie Olson
Description: Minneapolis, Minnesota : Abdo Publishing, 2021 | Series: Mighty muscle cars |
    Includes online resources and index
Identifiers: ISBN 9781532193262 (lib. bdg.) | ISBN 9781098211905 (ebook)
Subjects: LCSH: Muscle cars--Juvenile literature. | Motor vehicles--Juvenile literature. |
    Automobiles--Customizing--Juvenile literature. | Hot rods--Juvenile literature.
Classification: DDC 629.222--dc23

CONTENTS

OFF TO THE RACES

It's the final round of a drag race in Alamo, Texas. A Dodge Charger Daytona and a Dodge Challenger Scat Pack hum at the starting line. The green lights flash. Tires squeal. The cars are off!

The drivers race side by side. Just before the finish line, the Charger pulls ahead. Its driver clocks in at 7.98 seconds. The Charger has won!

DID YOU KNOW?

In a drag race, two cars race on a straight track called a drag strip. Most drag strips are one-eighth mile (0.2 km) or one-quarter mile (0.4 km) long.

AMERICAN MUSCLE

The Dodge Charger is one of the most iconic muscle cars on the market. Muscle cars are American high-performance cars. They are built for power and speed.

The first muscle car came out in 1949. Muscle cars soon became widely popular in the 1960s. They were made for drag racing. But most could also be driven on city streets.

DID YOU KNOW?

The drag race start light is called a Christmas tree. Yellow means wait. Green means go. And red means a driver started too early.

DODGE CHARGER FAST FACTS

Manufacturer: Chrysler

First model year: 1966

Top speed: 204 miles per hour (328 km/h)

Top horsepower: 717 hp

Top acceleration: 0 to 60 miles per hour
(96 km/h) in 3.4 seconds

MICHIGAN BORN

The Dodge Charger was born near Detroit, Michigan. In 1901, brothers Horace and John Dodge founded the Dodge Brothers Company in Detroit. In 1928, fellow Detroit automaker Walter Chrysler bought Dodge.

Chrysler produced **vehicles** for the US military in the 1940s. But as **World War II** ended, the company was ready to show off something fast and fun.

DID YOU KNOW?

The Dodge Brothers
Motor Company plant
was in Hamtramck,
Michigan, near Detroit.

A NEED FOR SPEED

In 1946, Chrysler introduced its first muscle car, the Dodge Charger. It was a **concept car**. But the public wasn't interested. So, the Charger had to wait.

By the 1960s, Americans were finally ready. Drag racing had become widely popular. So in 1966, Chrysler **debuted** the Charger. It was a perfect fit for drivers who valued performance and speed, both on the racetrack and on city streets!

The 1966 Dodge Charger came with a hemi engine. These engines have better airflow than others, making them more effective.

THE FIRST GENERATION

The 1966 Dodge Charger was based on another Dodge muscle car, the Coronet. But unlike the Coronet, the Charger was **designed** specifically for street racing.

Dodge wanted to build buzz around its new car. It entered the Charger into **NASCAR** races. The car was fast but hard to control. So, Dodge added a **spoiler** to the car.

A Charger is prepped for a race in Austin, Texas, in 1967.

CHANGING WITH THE TIMES

Dodge unveiled its second-**generation** Charger in 1968. It was a sports car with all the comforts of a **luxury car**. Sales of the 1968 Charger topped 90,000!

From 1971 to 1987, Dodge **debuted** three more generations of Chargers. During this time, the US made laws for automakers to reduce **pollution**. This made new Chargers less powerful. Sales dropped. Dodge stopped making Chargers in 1987.

The 1968 Charger was designed to flare out at the wheel arches. This "Coke bottle" frame was a popular style at the time.

BACK WITH A BANG

In 2006, the Charger came back in full force. The sixth-**generation** Charger returned to its racing roots. The new car was built for power and speed.

The car was so powerful that police officers started using them! The Charger was the fastest police car on US streets. Officers loved Chargers because they were comfortable too. The cars seemed ready for anything!

The Charger Pursuit model was created specifically for police use.

HELLCAT ON WHEELS

In 2015, Dodge released the Hellcat. This was the Charger's most powerful model yet. The Hellcat had more than 700 horsepower (hp). It could reach 60 miles per hour (96 km/h) in a few seconds! Dodge claimed it was the fastest mass-produced **sedan** in the world.

DID YOU KNOW?

Horsepower (hp) is a measure of how powerful an engine is. One hp equals the power needed to lift a 550-pound (249 kg) weight up one foot (0.3 m) in one second.

The Hellcat's speed and power means it burns fuel quickly. At top speeds, it can burn through a tank of gas in just 13 minutes!

UNDER THE HOOD

DODGE CHARGER HELLCAT

The 2019 Hellcat was the Charger's most powerful model to date. It came with a V8 engine. That means it had eight **cylinders**. Other Charger models have V6 engines. The more cylinders an engine has, the more powerful it is.

CAR ENGINES 101

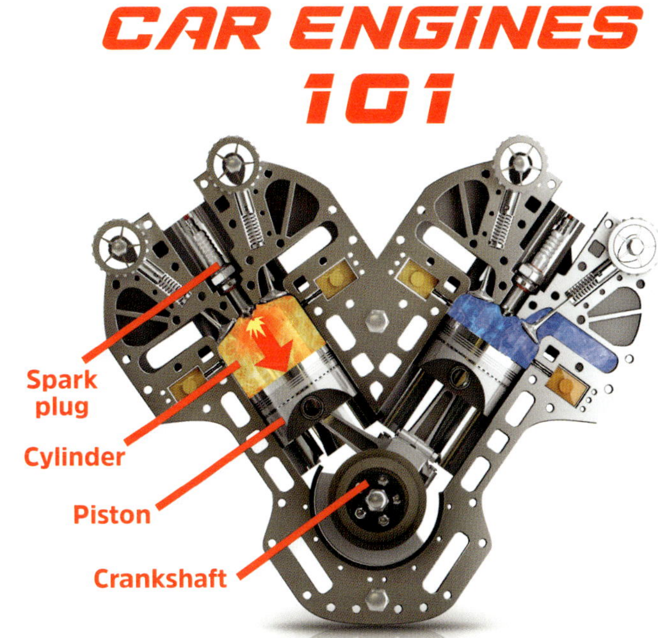

Car engines turn the energy in gasoline into motion. Fuel and air are pumped into the engine's **cylinders**. A spark creates an explosion. The explosion pushes the **piston** down to turn the **crankshaft**. This is a bit like a foot pushing down on a bicycle pedal. At high speed, these explosions happen thousands of times a minute!

RACING RECORDS

Over more than 50 years, the Charger has made a name for itself on the racetrack. For a while, it was unbeatable!

In 1969, the Dodge Charger Daytona model was the fastest **NASCAR** race car. In 1970, it became the first car to break 200 miles per hour (322 km/h) during a race. The Charger won so many races that NASCAR banned it in 1971. But the Charger is still a popular drag racing car!

The Daytona model featured a large spoiler.

CHARGERS ONSCREEN

Chargers have also found fame in movies and TV shows. In 1968, a Charger appeared in the movie *Bullitt*. A 1969 Charger known as "General Lee" appeared in the popular show *Dukes of Hazzard* from 1979 to 1985.

Starting in 2001, the Dodge Charger also appeared in the *Fast and Furious* films. Dominic, played by Vin Diesel, drives a **revamped** 1970 Dodge Charger.

The "General Lee" Charger performs a stunt jump in front of a crowd at the Detroit Autorama car show.

RACING TOWARD THE FUTURE

The Dodge Charger shows no signs of slowing down. The 2019 Charger featured more smart **technology** than ever before. New Chargers included touchscreens, voice command, and many more features.

Some Charger drivers are ready for the racetrack. Others will take the car on patrol. And some use the Charger to get to work and school. This muscle car has something for everyone!

A special model of the 2020 Charger honors the 1969 Charger Daytona. The new model clocks in at 717 horsepower!

TIMELINE

Horace and John Dodge started the Dodge Brothers Company.

1901

Chrysler released the Dodge Charger as a **concept car.**

1946

Dodge released its second-generation Charger.

1968

1928

Walter Chrysler purchased Dodge.

1966

Dodge released its first-**generation** Charger.

Dodge released its
fourth-generation
Charger.

Dodge released the
fifth-generation
Charger.

Dodge released the
Hellcat. This was
the Charger's most
powerful model yet.

1975

1982

2015

1971

2006

Dodge released its
third-**generation**
Charger.

Dodge released the
sixth-generation
Charger.

concept car—a car produced as a model to show a new style or technology but not made available for sale.

crankshaft—a long, metal rod that transfers energy from the engine through the transmission and eventually to the wheels.

cylinder—a shaft in which a piston of an engine moves.

debut—to present something for the first time.

design (dih-ZINE)—to plan how something will appear or work.

generation—a class of objects created from an earlier type.

luxury car—a car that provides drivers and other riders with a high level of comfort and quality.

NASCAR—the National Association for Stock Car Auto Racing.

piston—a part in an engine that moves up and down inside the cylinder.

pollution—human waste that dirties or harms air, water, or land.

revamp—to make something better or like new.

sedan—a four-door car that has front and back seats and can hold four or more people.

spoiler—a part at the rear of a car that prevents air flowing over the car from slipping under the car and lifting it up.

technology (tehk-NAH-luh-jee)—a capability given by the practical application of knowledge.

vehicle—something used for carrying persons or large objects. Some examples are cars, trucks, boats, and airplanes.

World War II—a war fought in Europe, Asia, and Africa from 1939 to 1945.

ONLINE RESOURCES

To learn more about the Dodge Charger, please visit **abdobooklinks.com** or scan this QR code. These links are routinely monitored and updated to provide the most current information available.